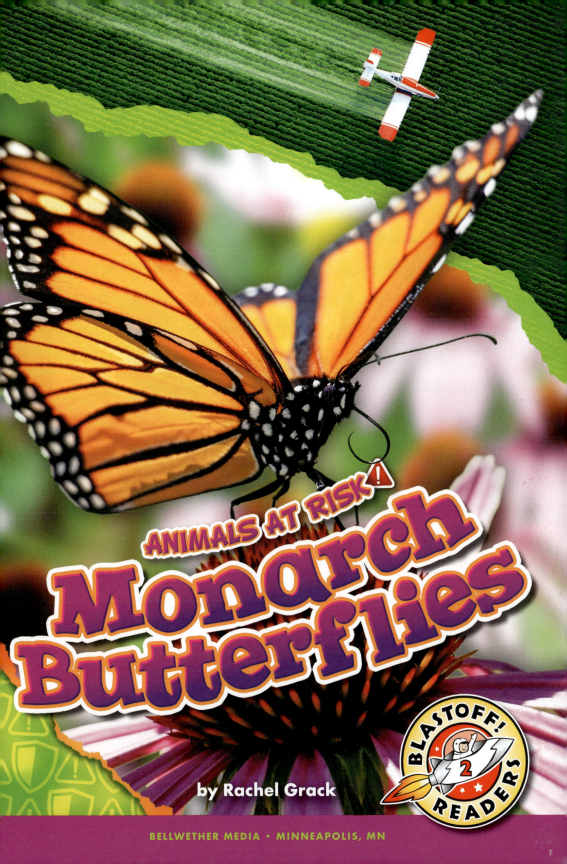

Blastoff! Readers are carefully developed by literacy experts to build reading stamina and move students toward fluency by combining standards-based content with developmentally appropriate text.

 Level 1 provides the most support through repetition of high-frequency words, light text, predictable sentence patterns, and strong visual support.

 Level 2 offers early readers a bit more challenge through varied sentences, increased text load, and text-supportive special features.

 Level 3 advances early-fluent readers toward fluency through increased text load, less reliance on photos, advancing concepts, longer sentences, and more complex special features.

★ **Blastoff! Universe**

Reading Level

Grade K

Grades 1–3

Grade 4

This edition first published in 2024 by Bellwether Media, Inc.

No part of this publication may be reproduced in whole or in part without written permission of the publisher. For information regarding permission, write to Bellwether Media, Inc., Attention: Permissions Department, 6012 Blue Circle Drive, Minnetonka, MN 55343.

Library of Congress Cataloging-in-Publication Data

Names: Koestler-Grack, Rachel A., 1973- author.
Title: Monarch butterflies / Rachel Grack.
Description: Minneapolis, MN : Bellwether Media, 2024. | Series: Blastoff! Readers. Animals at risk | Includes bibliographical references and index. | Audience: Ages 5-8 | Audience: Grades 2-3 | Summary: "Relevant images match informative text in this introduction to monarch butterflies. Intended for students in kindergarten through third grade"-- Provided by publisher.
Identifiers: LCCN 2023004264 (print) | LCCN 2023004265 (ebook) | ISBN 9798886874211 (library binding) | ISBN 9798886876093 (ebook)
Subjects: LCSH: Monarch butterfly--Juvenile literature. | Monarch butterfly--Conservation--Juvenile literature.
Classification: LCC QL561.N9 K64 2024 (print) | LCC QL561.N9 (ebook) | DDC 595.78/9--dc23/eng/20230130
LC record available at https://lccn.loc.gov/2023004264
LC ebook record available at https://lccn.loc.gov/2023004265

Text copyright © 2024 by Bellwether Media, Inc. BLASTOFF! READERS and associated logos are trademarks and/or registered trademarks of Bellwether Media, Inc.

Editor: Kieran Downs   Designer: Brittany McIntosh

Printed in the United States of America, North Mankato, MN.

Table of Contents

Far Fliers	4
In Danger!	8
Save the Monarch Butterflies!	12
Glossary	22
To Learn More	23
Index	24

Far Fliers

Monarch butterflies have orange and black wings. These **insects** are found in many countries.

But their numbers are falling. These butterflies are now **endangered**.

Most monarchs make long **migrations** every year. They need safe places to stop along the way.

But their **habitats** are being destroyed. People have caused most of their problems.

Migratory Monarch Butterfly Range

range =

In Danger!

Monarchs gather in trees in Mexico during winter. But forests are cleared for logging and farming.

Climate change also causes trouble. Colder winters are killing butterflies.

logging

Migratory Monarch Butterfly Stats

Least Concern | Near Threatened | Vulnerable | Endangered | Critically Endangered | Extinct in the Wild | Extinct

conservation status: endangered

life span: up to 9 months

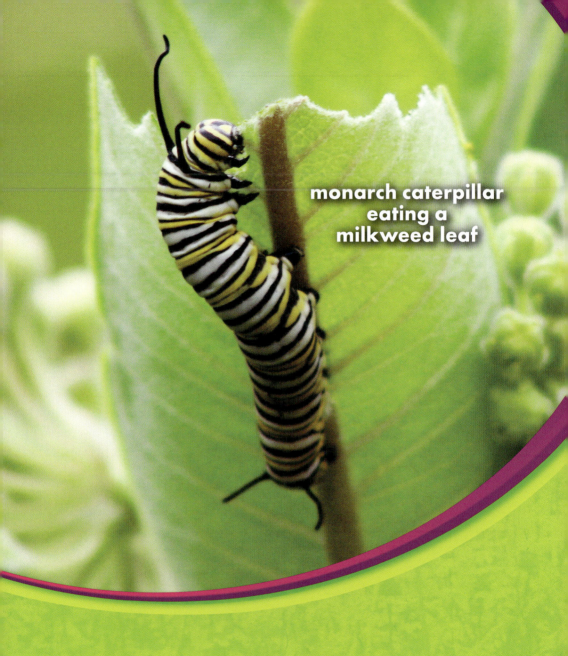

monarch caterpillar eating a milkweed leaf

Monarch caterpillars need milkweed leaves. It is the only food they eat.

But people use harmful plant sprays. These kill milkweeds. Caterpillars have trouble finding food.

Threats

1 people use plant sprays

2 milkweeds die

3 caterpillars have no food

Save the Monarch Butterflies!

Monarchs are important **pollinators**. They help many plants grow.

This provides food for other animals. Without the butterflies, wildlife would suffer.

The World with Monarch Butterflies

1. more monarch butterflies
2. plants grow
3. healthy wildlife

Governments **protect** land for monarchs. They save grasslands to give butterflies food.

They set aside forests as winter homes.

Wildlife workers plant milkweeds, trees, and flowers. Monarchs find food and resting spots.

They have places to lay their eggs.

eggs

People can grow **organic** gardens. They can avoid harmful plant sprays.

organic garden

This lets the butterflies land safely on plants and flowers.

Planting a flower garden with milkweeds helps monarchs.

Riding bikes instead of driving slows climate change. Together, everyone can save these beautiful butterflies!

planting milkweeds

Glossary

climate change—a human-caused change in Earth's weather due to warming temperatures

endangered—in danger of dying out

habitats—places and natural surroundings in which plants or animals live

insects—small animals with six legs and bodies divided into three parts

migrations—movements from one place to another, often with the seasons

organic—grown without using chemicals

pollinators—animals that spread pollen from one flower to another; pollen is a fine dust that helps plants make seeds.

protect—to keep safe

To Learn More

AT THE LIBRARY
Donnelly, Rebecca. *On the Move with Monarch Butterflies.* Minneapolis, Minn.: Jump!, 2023.

Hobbie, Ann. *Monarch Butterflies.* North Adams, Mass.: Storey Publishing, 2021.

Schuetz, Kari. *Monarch Butterfly Migration.* Minneapolis, Minn.: Bellwether Media, 2019.

ON THE WEB

FACTSURFER

Factsurfer.com gives you a safe, fun way to find more information.

1. Go to www.factsurfer.com.

2. Enter "monarch butterflies" into the search box and click 🔍.

3. Select your book cover to see a list of related content.

Index

caterpillars, 10, 11
climate change, 8, 20
colors, 4
eggs, 17
endangered, 5
farming, 8
flowers, 16, 19, 20
food, 10, 11, 13, 14, 16
forests, 8, 15
gardens, 18, 20
governments, 14
grasslands, 14
habitats, 7
insects, 4
land, 14
logging, 8
Mexico, 8
migrations, 6
milkweeds, 10, 11, 16, 20
numbers, 5
people, 7, 11, 18

plants, 11, 12, 19
pollinators, 12
range, 7
sprays, 11, 18
stats, 9
threats, 11
trees, 8, 16
ways to help, 20
wildlife, 13
wildlife workers, 16
wings, 4
winter, 8, 15
world with, 13

The images in this book are reproduced through the courtesy of: Annette Shaff, front cover; Butterfly Hunter, p. 3; Parry Photography, p. 4; RukiMedia, p. 5; Manuel Balesteri, p. 6; Eduardo Cota, p. 8; Joel Trick, pp. 8-9; Piper333, p. 10; Gavin Baker Photography, p. 10 (top left); Eleanor Kiwano/ Alamy Stock Photo, p. 10 (top right); Luciano de la Rosa, p. 10 (bottom); Media Marketing, p. 12; Shawn Einerson, p. 13 (top left); Hecos, p.13 (top right); Cynthia Sliman, p. 13 (bottom); Jean-Maurice Cormier, p. 14; Noradoa, p. 15; Richard Ellis/ Alamy Stock Photo, p. 16; Survivalphotos/ Alamy Stock Photo, p. 17 (top); K Quinn Ferris, p. 17 (bottom); Irina Fischer, p. 18; Geri Lynn Smith, p. 19; Nature and Science/ Alamy Stock Photo, p. 20; Candy_Plus, pp. 20-21; ulrich missbach, p. 22.